Yes, Cubs!

by Luisa Soto

Here is a mom.

Here come the cubs.

A mom can get nuts.

Cubs get bugs. Yum!

Mom can see a den.

Mom and the cubs go in.

Mom and the cubs nap.

Is Mom up yet? Yes!

The cubs get up.

The cubs run and dig.

Cubs can dig for yams.

Did you see the cubs?

Did you see a mom? Yes!